Healing Days

A Guide for Kids Who Have Experienced Trauma

by Susan Farber Straus, PhD
illustrated by Maria Bogade

Magination Press • Washington, DC
American Psychological Association

With love and appreciation to Mom, Dad, Marilyn, Rebecca, Emily, Charlotte, Evan, Zach, and of course, David.

This book is dedicated to the safety and well-being of all children. —S.F.S.

To my wonderful friend Zeljka. It is a blessing to know you and have you in my life. And to my children, thank you so much for being my greatest inspiration. —M.B.

Published by
MAGINATION PRESS
An Educational Publishing Foundation Book
American Psychological Association
750 First Street, NE
Washington, DC 20002

For more information about our books, including a complete catalog, please write to us, call 1-800-374-2721, or visit our website at www.apa.org/pubs/magination.

Printed by Phoenix Color Corporation, Hagerstown, MD

Library of Congress Cataloging-in-Publication Data
Straus, Susan Farber.
  Healing days : a guide for kids who have experienced trauma / by Susan Farber Straus, PhD ; illustrated by Maria Bogade.
    pages cm
  Audience: 6–11.
  ISBN 978-1-4338-1292-7 (hardcover : alk. paper) — ISBN 978-1-4338-1293-4 (pbk. : alk. paper) 1. Psychic trauma in children —Treatment — Juvenile literature. 2. Post-traumatic stress disorder in children—Treatment — Juvenile literature. I. Bogade, Maria, illustrator. II. Title.
  RJ506.P66S77 2013
  618.92'8521—dc23
                          2012035872
Manufactured in the United States of America

First printing April 2013

10 9 8 7 6 5 4 3 2 1

Note to Readers

When bad and scary things happen to kids, their world turns upside down. Nothing seems the same. Nothing seems right. This is a book for you and other kids who have had something bad and scary happen. You can read this book with your therapist or another grown-up, or you can read it by yourself. It will help you to see that you're not alone, and that the same kind of thing happens to other boys and girls, too. You may not realize this, but you are very brave for telling a grown-up what happened. This is the very first step towards helping yourself feel better.

The book you are about to read tells about the feelings, thoughts, and behaviors that many kids have after a bad and scary thing happens. While you are reading this book, if you feel like it, you can talk about your own feelings and thoughts, too. Some of your feelings and thoughts may be the same as those of the kids in this book. Others may be different.

One thing that lots of kids worry about is whether they are to blame for the bad thing that happened. Lots of kids believe they are bad because of their angry feelings and behavior. Maybe you worry about these things too. This book will help you to see that you are a good kid and are not to blame. This book will also help you to learn some of the ways you can help yourself feel safer, more relaxed, and confident. Getting better takes time and hard work, but you can do it! Lots of good people will be there to help you along the way.

Best,
Susan Farber Straus

Something bad happened to me. I did not want anyone to know. I was scared. I was sad. I was angry. I was embarrassed. I was hurt and confused. I tried to forget. I tried to sleep and not wake up. I tried to think it wasn't me it happened to. I tried to turn off the pictures in my head. I tried to numb the feelings and quiet the noises I heard.

I even tried to stop the hurt by hurting myself...and hurting others. Everything reminded me.

Sometimes I felt like the bad thing was happening all over again. Sometimes I got very nervous and jumpy. Sometimes I didn't even want to go places or do things that reminded me of the bad thing.

My dreams scared me. The dark scared me.
I had trouble sleeping and my tummy hurt.

I wanted to hold onto Auntie tight and never let go. I cried a lot, and did other things I hadn't done since I was a baby.

My teacher said I wasn't focusing, I wasn't working, I was distracted, and I wasn't playing nicely.

I was getting into trouble. But I didn't care about school···or anything else.

My friends said I wasn't fun. My friends said I was acting weird. My friends didn't know my secret. I felt like I couldn't tell anyone about it. I felt so lonely.

I thought I was bad. I thought everyone was looking at me and thinking, "bad kid." I thought no one liked me anymore. I didn't know what to do.

But my auntie knew. She took me to see a therapist. Auntie explained that a therapist is a nice person who understands all about kids.

I drew some pictures for my therapist. I played with her toys. I talked and even answered some hard questions.

My therapist listened very carefully. We talked
about the thing that happened to me. She said it
happens to other kids, too. She said they were good
kids, like me. It wasn't their fault. But they felt
the same things I felt and they were hurt too.

My therapist reminded me of some things I had forgotten. Like most people are good and won't hurt kids. Like I'm a brave kid because I told. Sometimes secrets need to be told.

That my friends will still like me if I treat them nicely, like I want them to treat me. That my dog will still like me if I treat him with love. That children are not responsible for how adults act. That things will get better after a while.

My therapist taught me that when people and animals are hurt, scared, or stressed, their bodies react. They prepare for danger and that's a good thing, some of the time. Here's what animals do when they get scared and are in danger:

- Fight

- Run away or "take flight"

- Stay very still or "freeze"

My therapist says that "fight, flight, or freeze" explains why when something bad or scary happens, our muscles get tense, as if our bodies were getting ready to fight.

Our hearts race, and our breathing speeds up, as if we were going to run away.

Or our bodies can't move, and our brains block out our thoughts and feelings, as if we were frozen.

My therapist told me that after a bad thing happens, it's natural for our bodies and our minds to keep acting like the danger is still there, even when it's not. But that's not always helpful.
You can get tired trying to watch out for danger and not have the energy to have fun or learn in school.

Like when I felt too tired to play with my friends and just wanted to sleep.

You can begin thinking that everyone, even your friends, are out to hurt you and really they're not. Like when my best friend bumped into me in line ...

... and I pushed him back.

You can get worried that everyone is staring at you when really that's not true either. Like when I dropped my juicebox, and I heard some kids laugh.

I felt so ashamed that I ran into the bathroom and cried.

So my therapist helped me find ways to feel better and safer. Now, I have a safety plan if I ever think I am in danger.

My Safety Plan:

• Talk to these trusted people:

Auntie
Granny

• Call this phone number:

Auntie 555-0100

I also have a feel-good plan that helps keep my feelings under control.

My Feel-Good plan:

- Exercise.

- Practice deep breathing.

- Relax my muscles.

- Do fun activities that I enjoy, like yoga, drawing, or listening to happy music.

- Create a calming bedtime routine.

- Get together with friends.

I exercise by riding my bike, playing sports, taking a walk, or walking the dog. I try to do something every day.

I practice deep breathing as soon as I start to feel nervous or afraid.

First, I take a long, deep breath through my nose, feeling my tummy rise as I breathe in. I like to pretend I'm smelling a delicious chocolate birthday cake. Then I hold the breath for a second or two.

Then, I slowly breathe out through my mouth, just like I'm blowing out the birthday candles in one long, slow breath. I can repeat this as often as I need to until my body starts to feel more relaxed.

Muscle relaxing felt silly at first, but I practiced it anyway.
First, I tighten the muscles in my feet, curling my toes. I count to ten and then relax those muscles.

Next, I tighten the muscles in my lower legs, count to ten and relax. I keep doing this with all the muscles in my body (saving my eyes and nose for last) until my whole body feels relaxed. It helps me fall asleep at night.

I even tried it at school before a test, and guess what? It helped me think!

I go with Auntie to yoga. In yoga we learn different stretches and how to control our breath. I got to be really good at standing on my head. (Better than Auntie!)

I made a list of things to do every night before bed. Instead of watching TV or a movie, which could be scary, I gather my favorite stuffed animals into bed, read a story,

get a goodnight hug,

get tucked in, have my nightlight turned on, and get wished "sweet dreams." It helps me sleep.

I worked at treating people nicely and respecting their feelings, and I remembered how much fun it is to have friends. My therapist told me that I've been a good kid all along, but it took me a while to believe her. Now I know she's right.

She also told me it sometimes takes
a while but I can be a happy kid
again, a happy good kid.
I'm beginning to think she's right
about that too.

Susan Farber Straus, PhD, is a clinical child psychologist who has worked for the past twenty-four years with young trauma victims, many of whom have been physically, sexually, or emotionally abused. Following her education at Cornell University and Ohio State, and internship at McLean Hospital, she worked in both private practice and residential treatment settings. She is currently Senior Psychologist at Catholic Charities Child and Family Services in Baltimore, Maryland. She and her husband have two daughters, now grown, and a granddaughter, age four.

Maria Bogade is an illustrator who creates her own unique environments and appealing characters to entertain children and adults alike. She also illustrated the Magination Press book *Ben's Flying Flowers*.

Magination Press publishes self-help books for kids and the adults in their lives. Magination Press is an imprint of the American Psychological Association, the largest scientific and professional organization representing psychologists in the United States.